EASY GUITAR
WITH NOTES & TAB

CHART
OF 2012-2013

MW01173820

ISBN 978-1-4803-3809-8

HAL•LEONARD®
CORPORATION
7777 W. BLUEMOUND RD. P.O. BOX 13819 MILWAUKEE, WI 53213

Visit Hal Leonard Online at
www.halleonard.com

The A Team

Words and Music by Ed Sheeran

*Capo II

Strum Pattern: 3
Pick Pattern: 3

Intro
Moderately slow, in 2

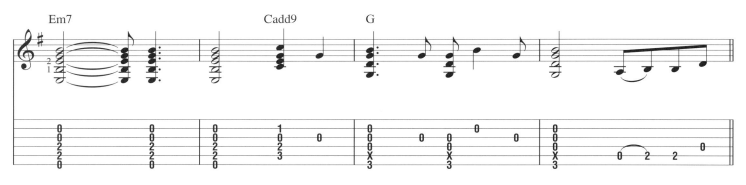

*Optional: To match recording, place capo at 2nd fret.

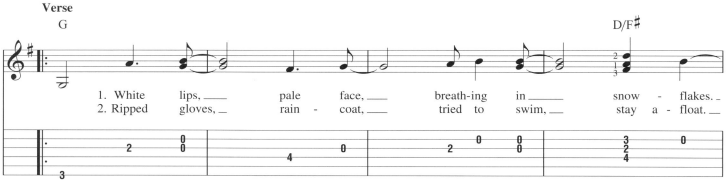

Verse

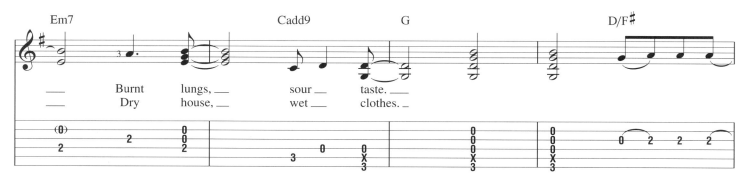

1. White lips, ___ pale face, ___ breath-ing in ___ snow - flakes. ___
2. Ripped gloves, _ rain - coat, _ tried to swim, _ stay a - float. _

Burnt lungs, ___ sour ___ taste. ___
Dry house, _ wet ___ clothes. _

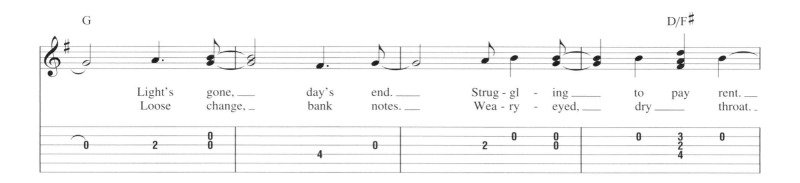

Light's gone, ___ day's end. ___ Strug - gl - ing ___ to pay rent. ___
Loose change, ___ bank notes. ___ Wea - ry - eyed, ___ dry ___ throat. ___

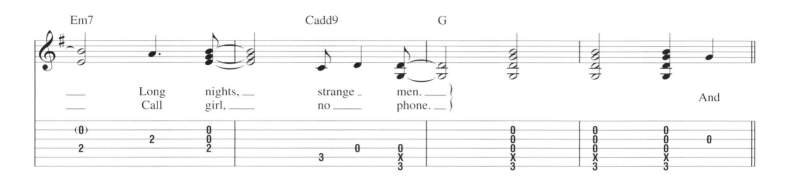

___ Long nights, ___ strange ___ men. ___
___ Call girl, ___ no ___ phone. ___

And

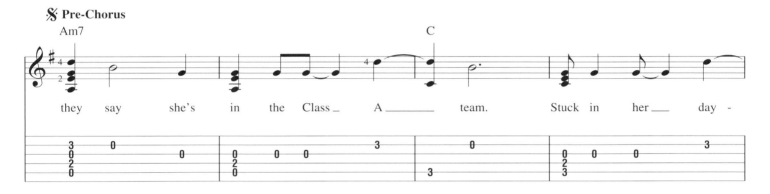

Pre-Chorus

they say she's in the Class ___ A ___ team. Stuck in her ___ day -

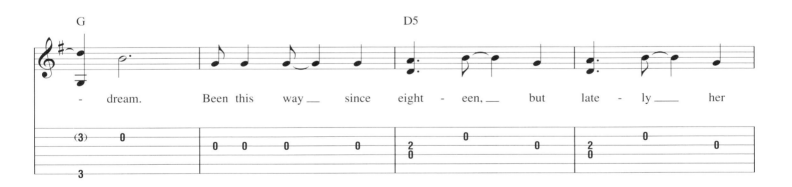

- dream. Been this way ___ since eight - een, ___ but late - ly ___ her

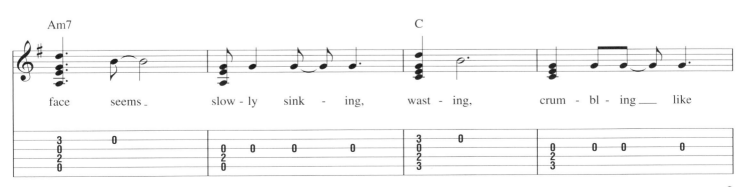

face seems ___ slow - ly sink - ing, wast - ing, crum - bl - ing ___ like

3

Chorus

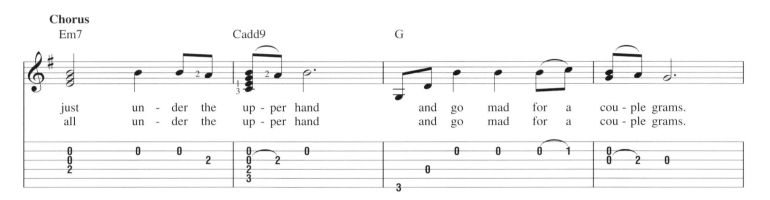

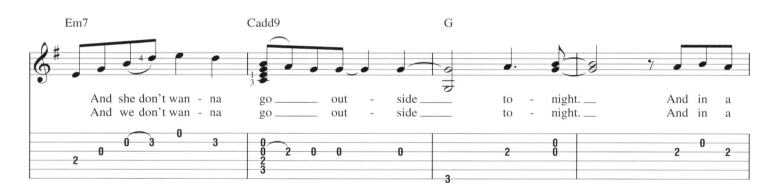

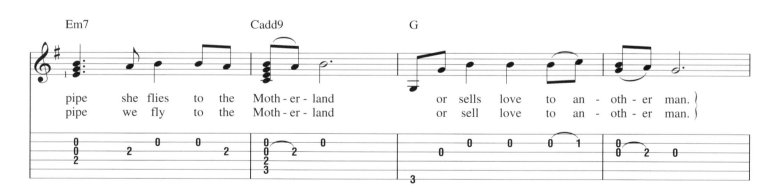

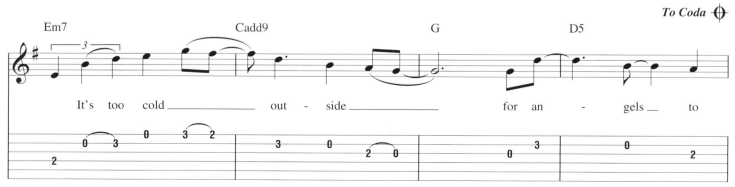

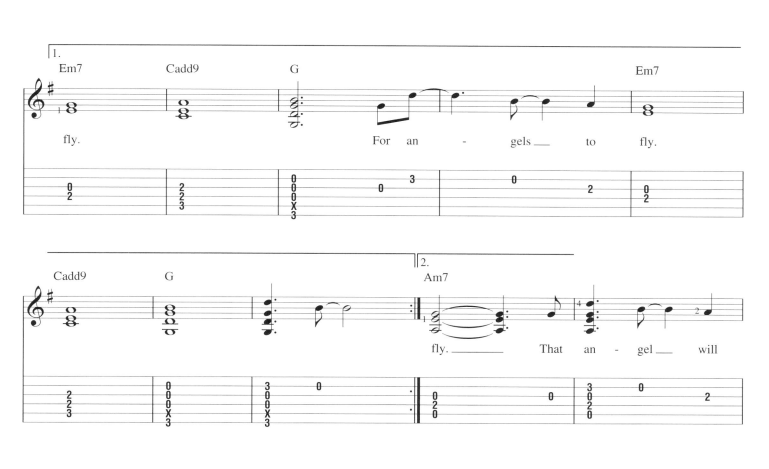

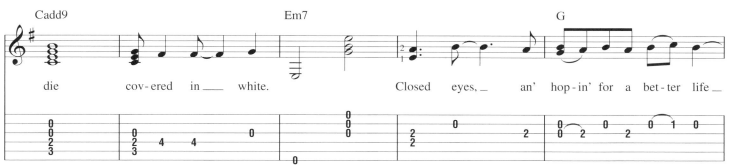

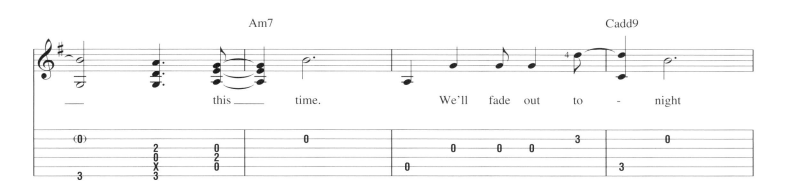

Interlude

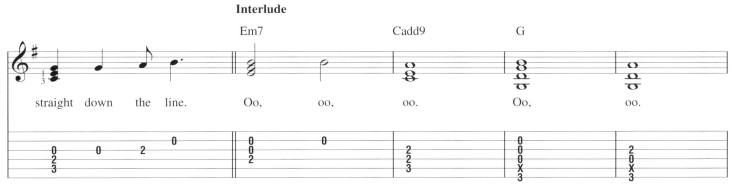

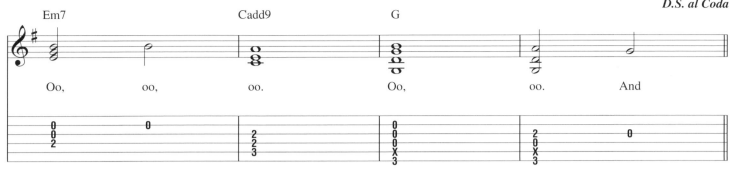

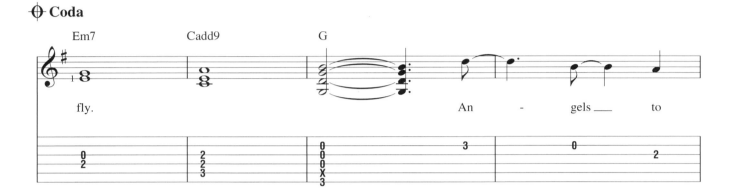

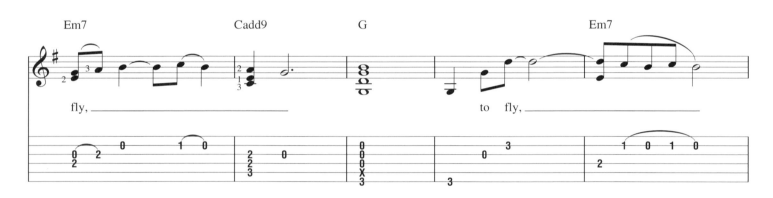

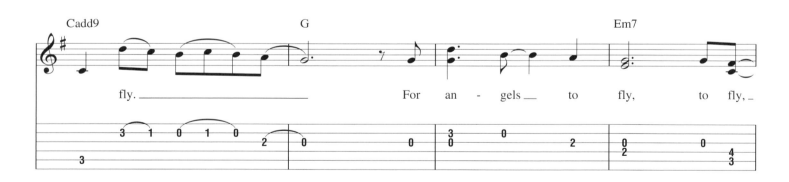

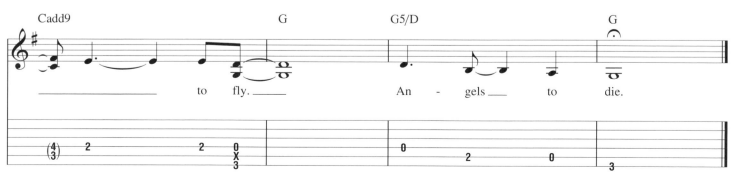

Home

Words and Music by Greg Holden and Drew Pearson

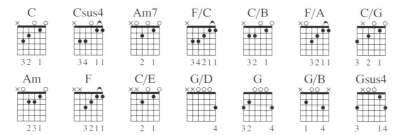

Strum Pattern: 1
Pick Pattern: 5

Intro
Moderately, in 2

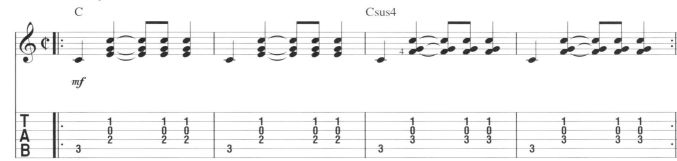

Verse

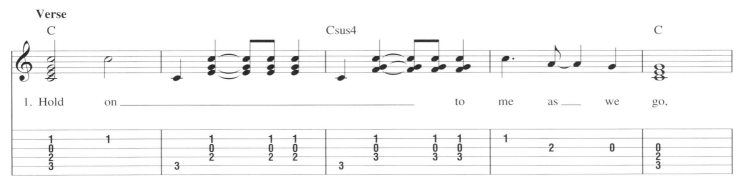

1. Hold on to me as we go,

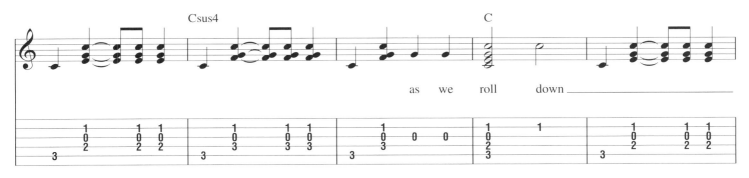

as we roll down

this un-fa-mil-iar road.

And al - though this wave _____

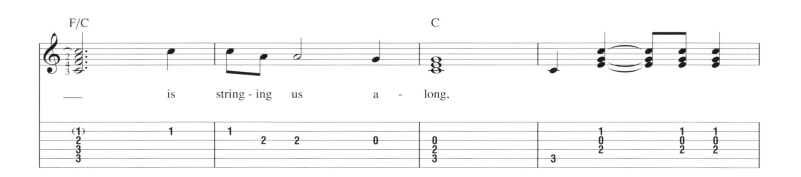

_____ is string - ing us a - long,

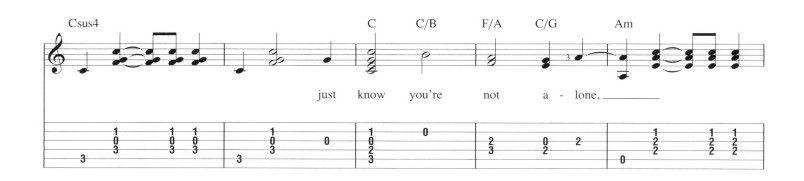

just know you're not a - lone, _____

'cause I'm gon - na make this place your _____

_____ home.

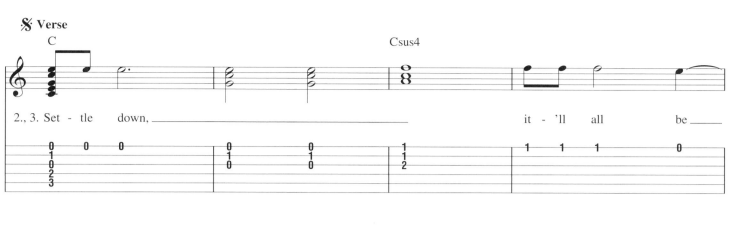

2., 3. Set - tle down, _____ it - 'll all be _____

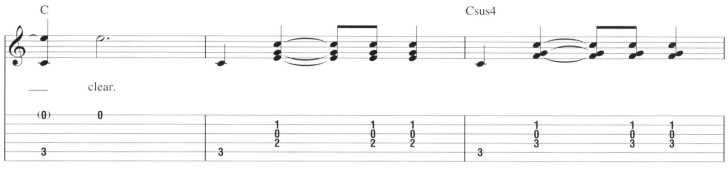

___ clear.

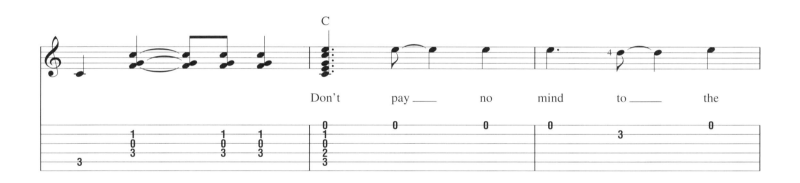

Don't pay ___ no mind to _____ the

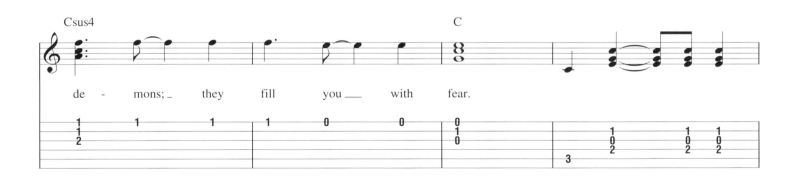

de - mons; _ they fill you ___ with fear.

Trou - ble, ___ it

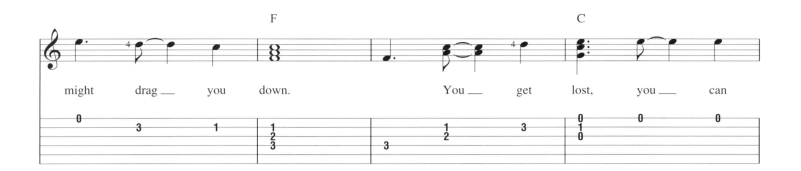

might drag — you down. You — get lost, you — can

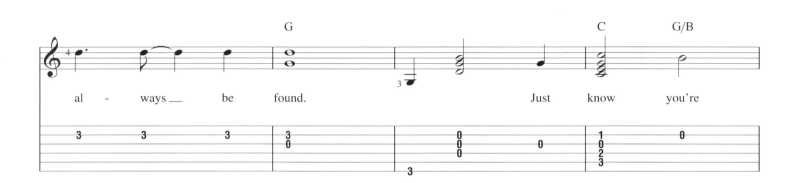

al - ways — be found. Just know you're

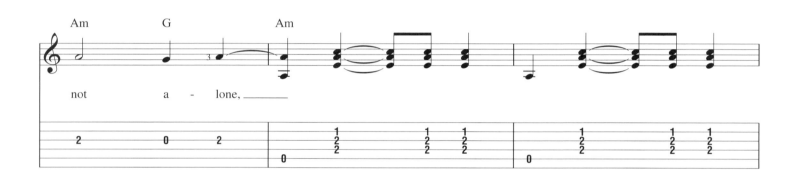

not a - lone, _____

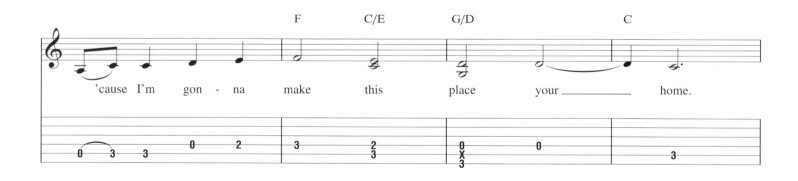

'cause I'm gon - na make this place your _____ home.

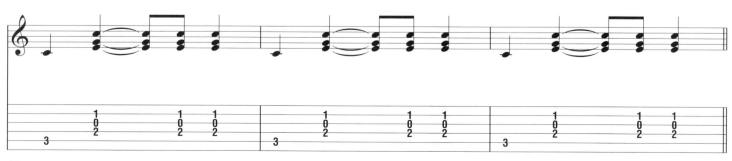

Interlude

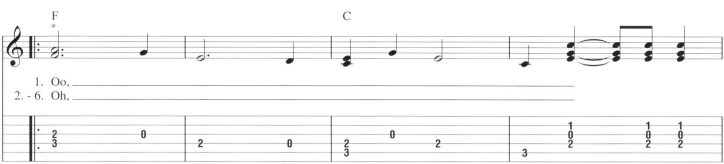

*Sung one octave higher, next 13 meas.

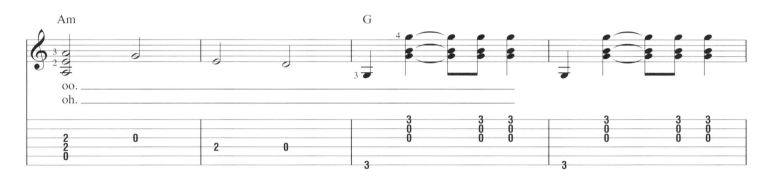

6th time, To Coda ⊕

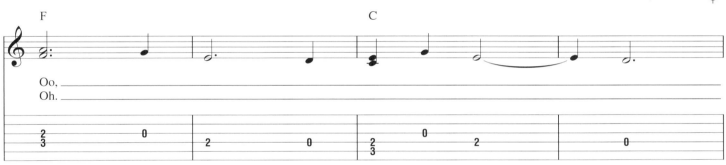

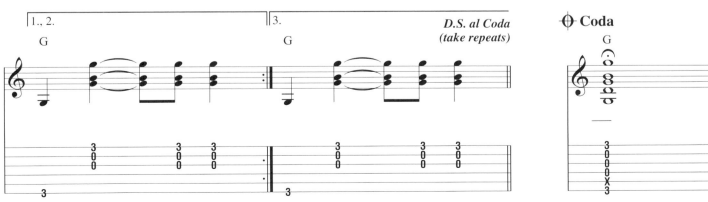

Diamonds

Words and Music by Sia Furler, Tor Hermansen, Mikkel Eriksen and Benjamin Levin

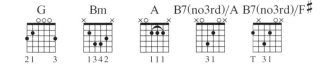

Strum Pattern: 3
Pick Pattern: 3

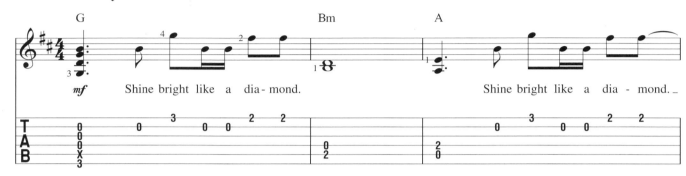

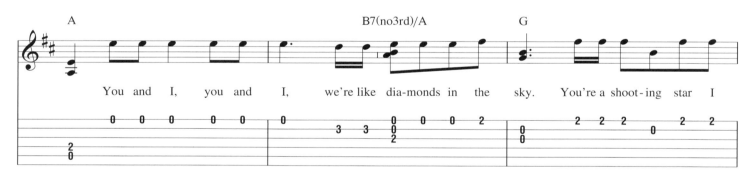

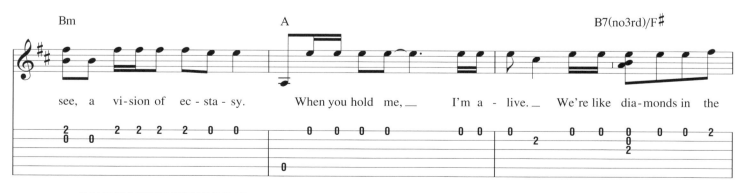

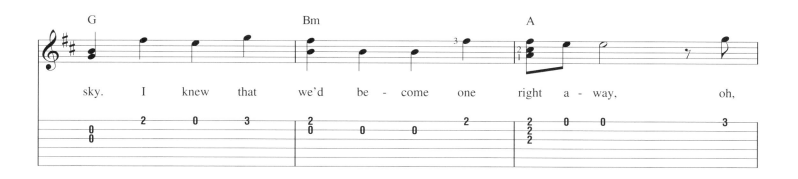

sky. I knew that we'd be - come one right a - way, oh,

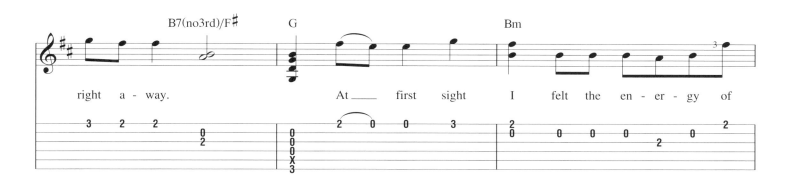

right a - way.   At ___ first sight I felt the en - er - gy of

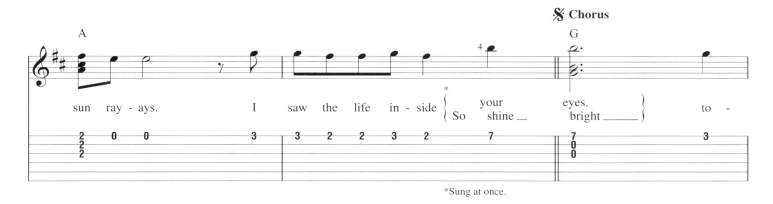

Chorus

sun ray - ays.   I saw the life in - side { So your shine ___ eyes. bright ___ } to -

*Sung at once.

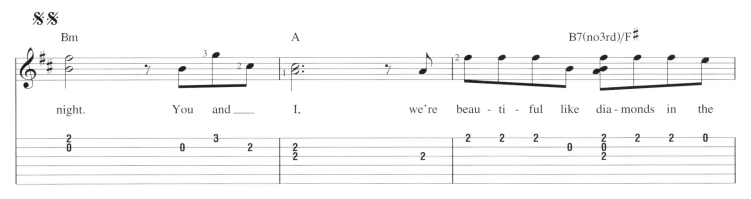

night.   You and ___ I, we're beau - ti - ful like dia - monds in the

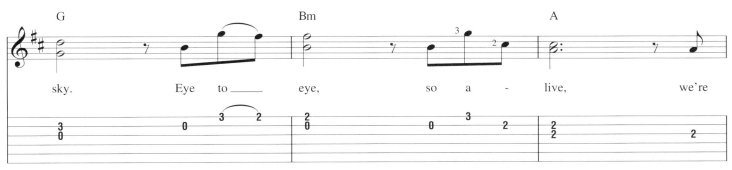

sky.   Eye to ___ eye, so a - live, we're

13

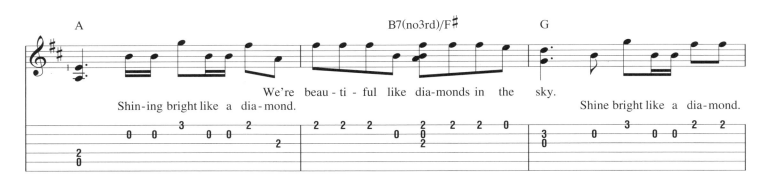

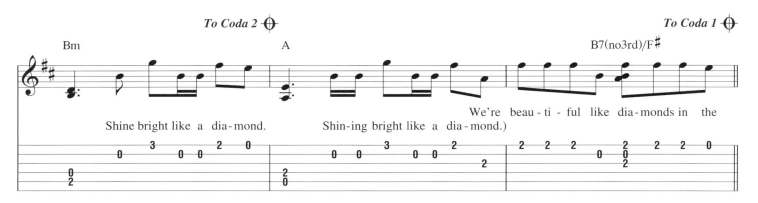

Verse

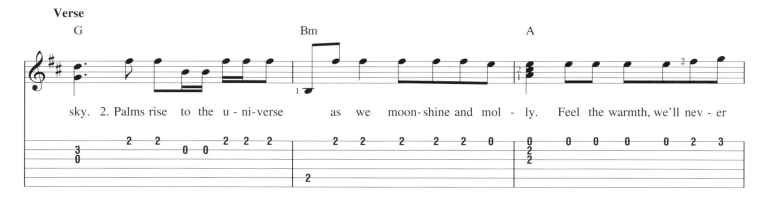

When you hold me, __ I'm a - live. __ We're like dia-monds in the sky. At __ first sight

D.S. al Coda 1

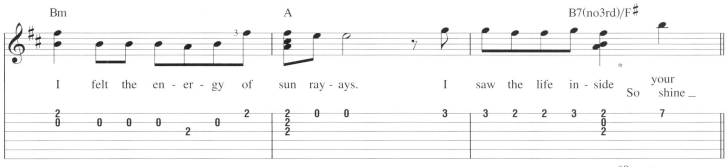

I felt the en - er - gy of sun ray - ays. I saw the life in - side So your shine __

*Sung at once.

Coda 1

sky. Shine bright like a dia - mond. Shine bright like a dia - mond.

D.S.S. al Coda 2

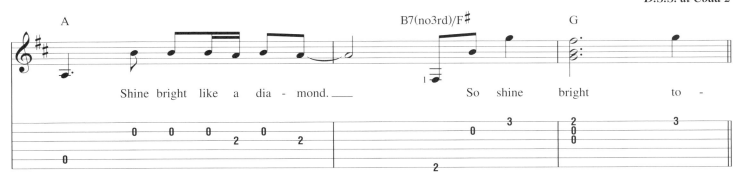

Shine bright like a dia - mond. __ So shine bright to -

Coda 2

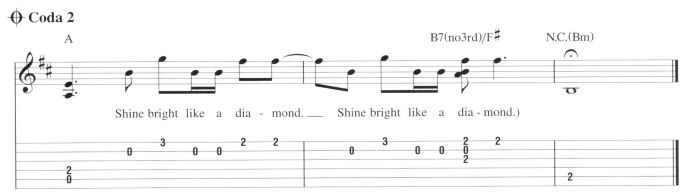

Shine bright like a dia - mond. __ Shine bright like a dia - mond.)

15

Die Young

Words and Music by Kesha Sebert, Benjamin Levin, Lukasz Gottwald, Henry Walter and Nate Ruess

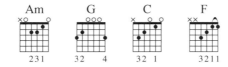

*Capo IV

Strum Pattern: 1
Pick Pattern: 1

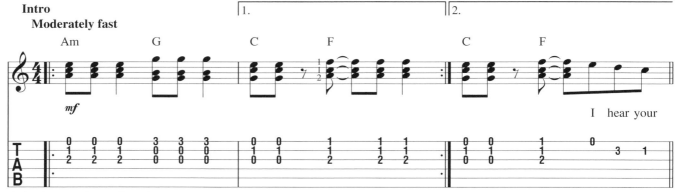

*Optional: To match recording, place capo at 4th fret.

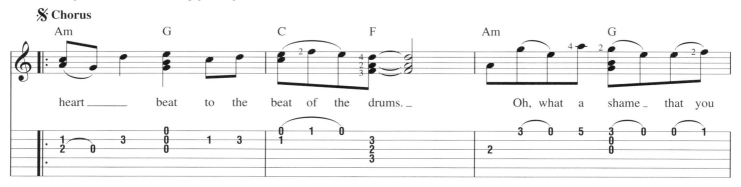

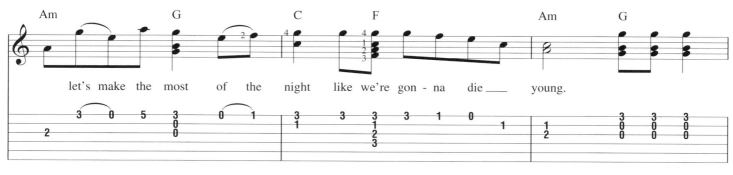

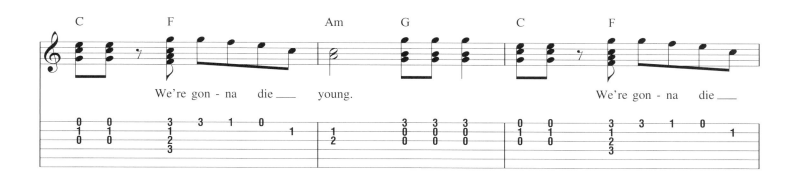

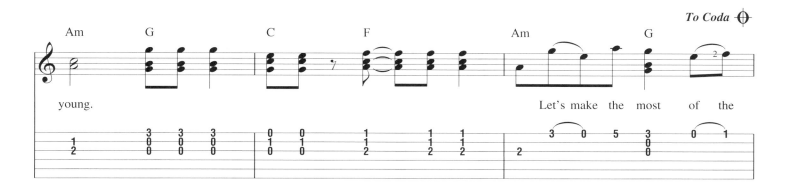

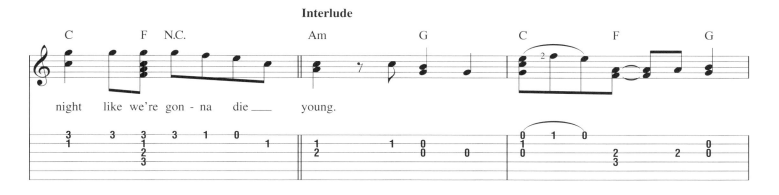

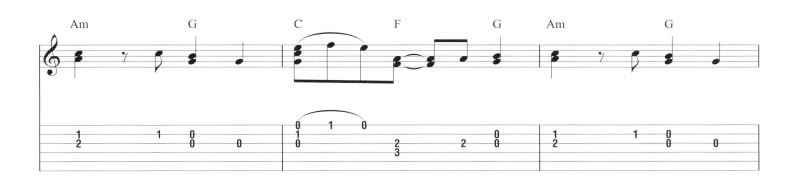

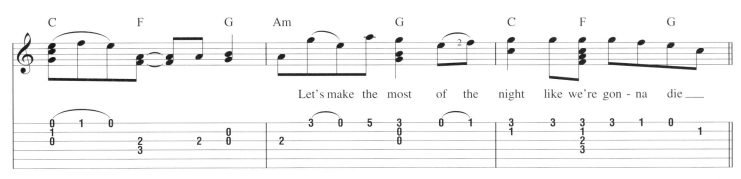

Verse

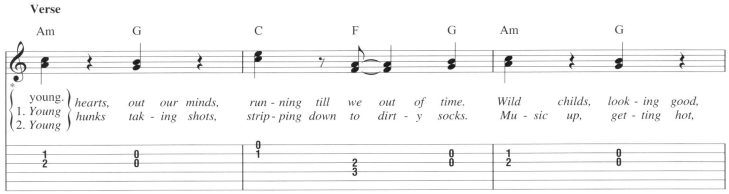

*Sung at once. Lyrics in italics are spoken throughout.

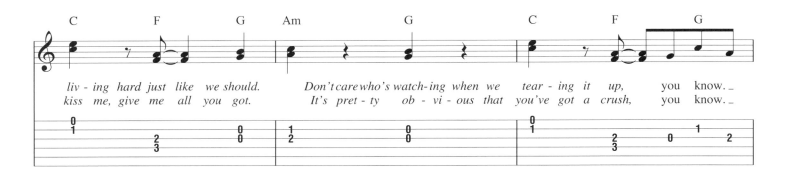

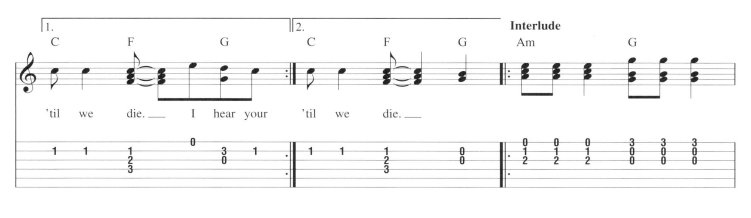

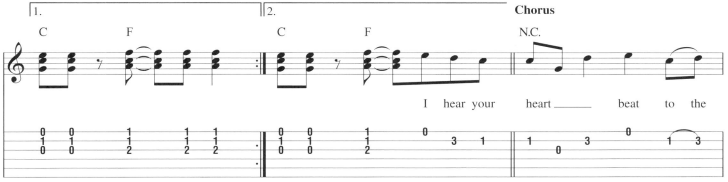

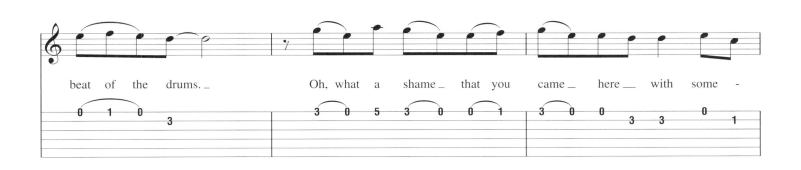

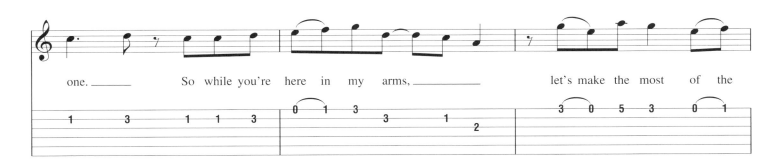

D.S. al Coda   ⊕ **Coda**

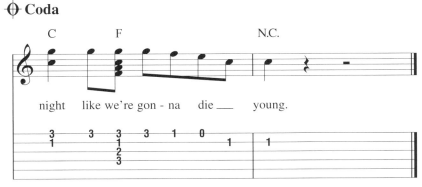

*Sung at once.

Ho Hey

Words and Music by Jeremy Fraites and Wesley Schultz

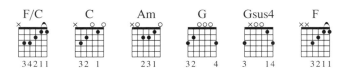

Strum Pattern: 5
Pick Pattern: 1

Intro
Moderately slow, in 2

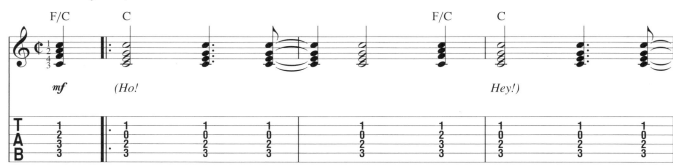

Verse

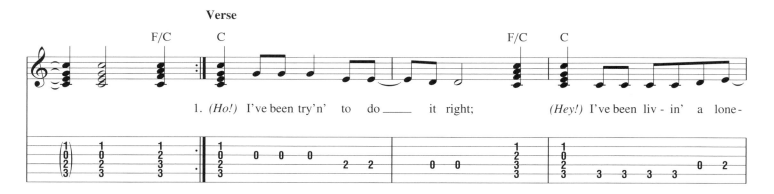

1. (Ho!) I've been try'n' to do ___ it right; (Hey!) I've been liv - in' a lone-

- ly life. _____ (Ho!) I've been sleep - in' here ___ in - stead;

(Hey!) I've been sleep - in' in ___ my bed, _____ (Ho!) I've been sleep - in' in ___

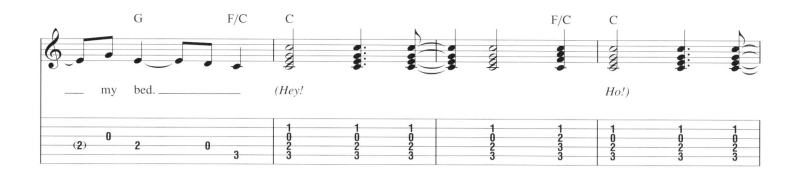

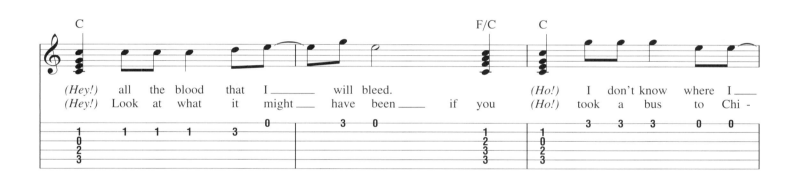

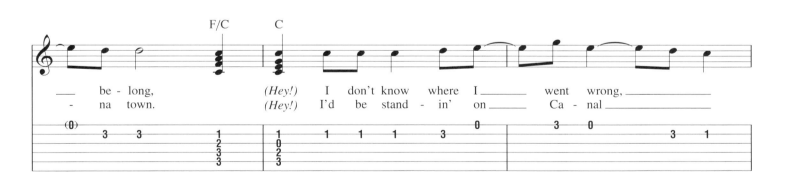

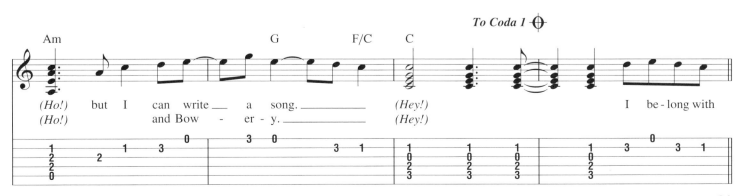

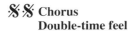

Chorus
Double-time feel

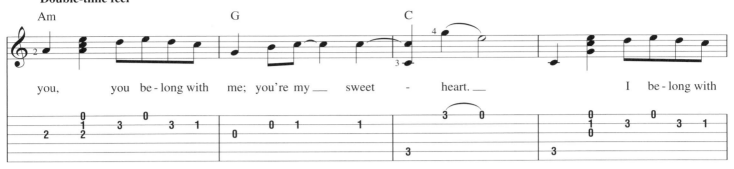

you,   you be - long with   me; you're my ___ sweet - heart. ___   I be - long with

End double-time feel

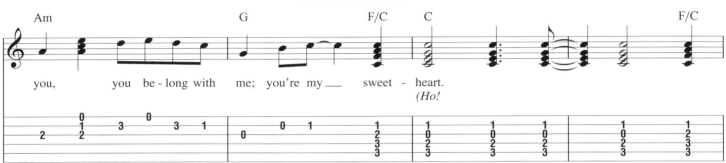

you,   you be - long with   me; you're my ___ sweet - heart.
(Ho!

To Coda 2

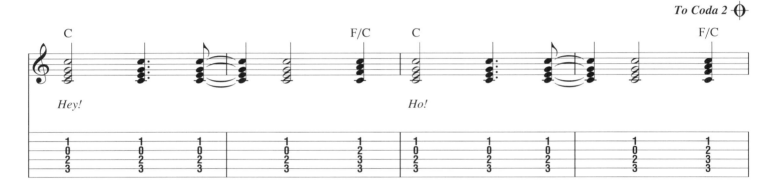

Hey!   *Ho!*

D.S. al Coda 1   **Coda 1**

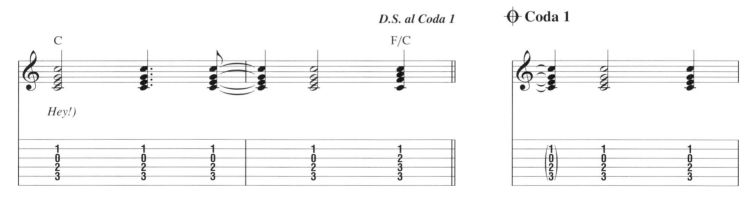

Hey!)

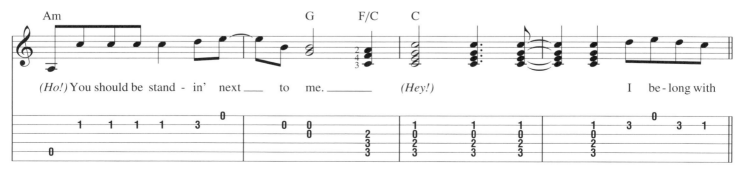

(Ho!) You should be stand - in' next ___ to me. _____ *(Hey!)*   I be - long with

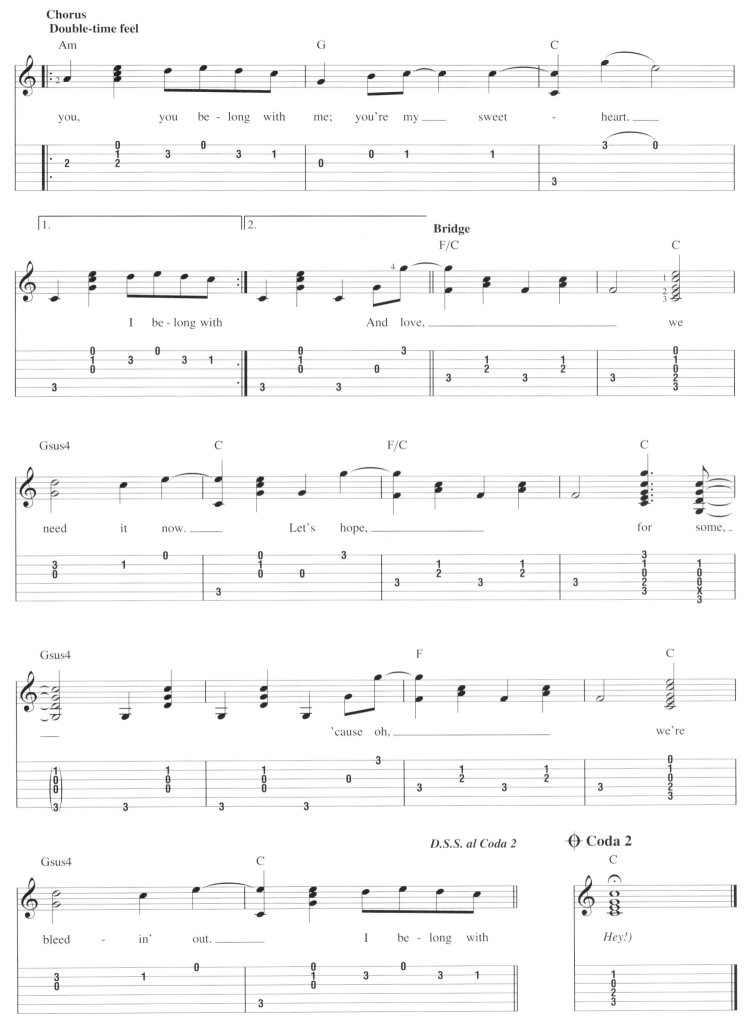

It's Time

Words and Music by Daniel Reynolds, Benjamin McKee and Daniel Sermon

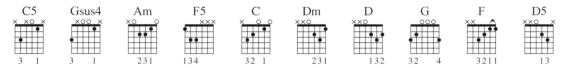

*Capo II

Strum Pattern: 5
Pick Pattern: 5

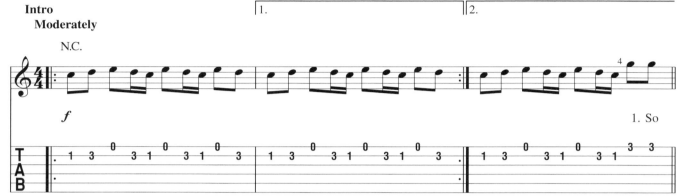

*Optional: To match recording, place capo at 2nd fret.

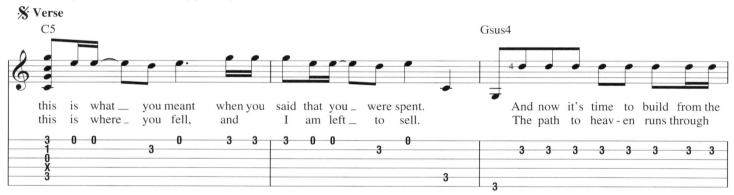

this is what __ you meant   when you said that you __ were spent.   And now it's time to build from the
this is where __ you fell,   and   I am left __ to sell.   The path to heav-en runs through

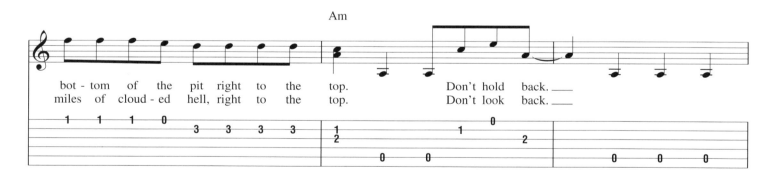

bot-tom of the pit right to the top.   Don't hold   back. __
miles of cloud-ed hell, right to the top.   Don't look   back. __

Pack-ing my bags, and giv-ing the A-cad-e-my a rain - check.}
Turn-ing to rags, and giv-ing the com-mod-i-ties a rain - check.}

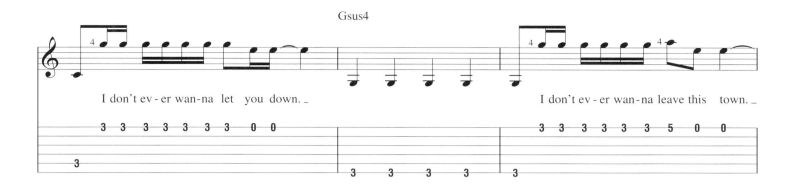

Gsus4

I don't ev-er wan-na let you down. _

I don't ev-er wan-na leave this town. _

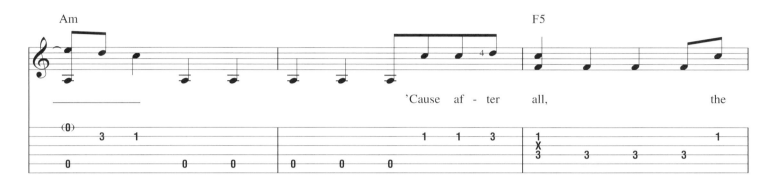

Am

F5

'Cause af - ter all, the

𝄋 𝄋 **Chorus**

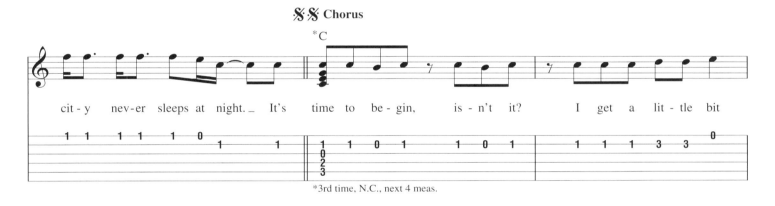

*C

cit - y nev-er sleeps at night. _ It's time to be - gin, is - n't it? I get a lit - tle bit

*3rd time, N.C., next 4 meas.

Am

Dm

big - ger, but then, I'll ad - mit, I'm just the same as I was. _

To Coda 1 ⊕

To Coda 2 ⊕

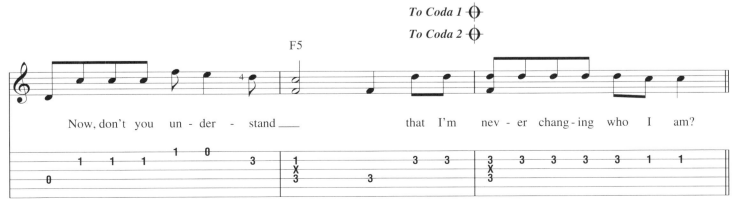

F5

Now, don't you un - der - stand ___ that I'm nev - er chang - ing who I am?

Interlude

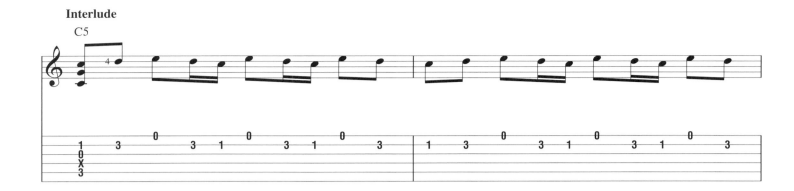

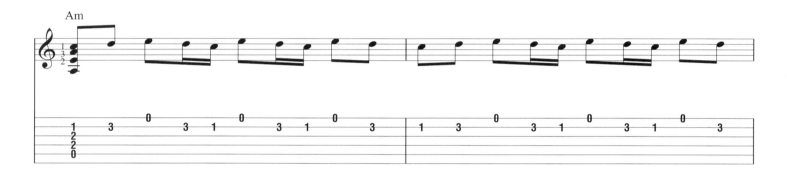

D.S. al Coda 1

2. So

✪ Coda 1

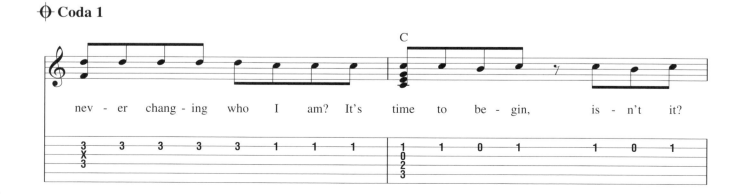

nev - er chang - ing who I am? It's time to be - gin, is - n't it?

Bridge

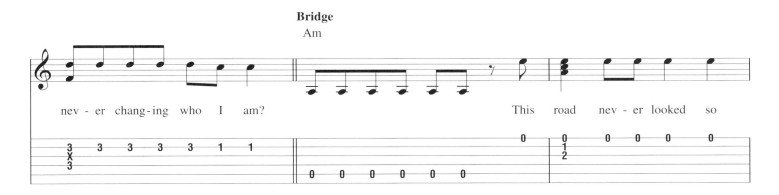

D.S.S. al Coda 2

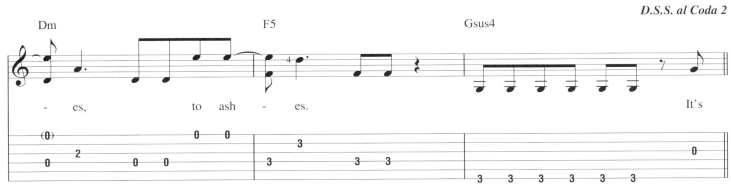

⊕ Coda 2

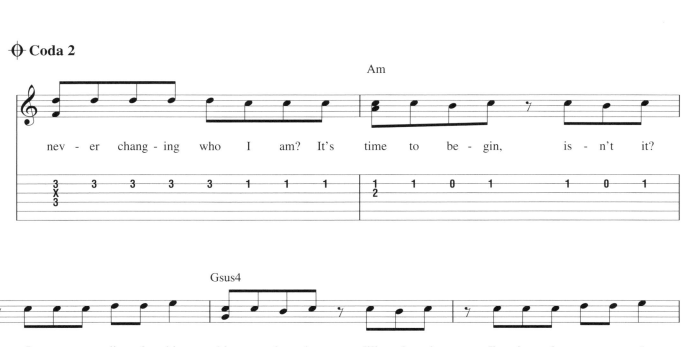

nev - er chang - ing who I am? It's time to be - gin, is - n't it?

I get a lit - tle bit big - ger, but then, I'll ad - mit, I'm just the same as I

was. _____ Now, don't you un - der - stand _____ that I'm

Outro

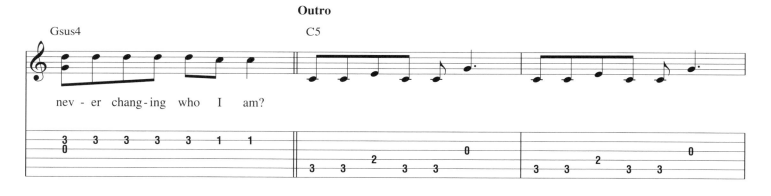

nev - er chang - ing who I am?

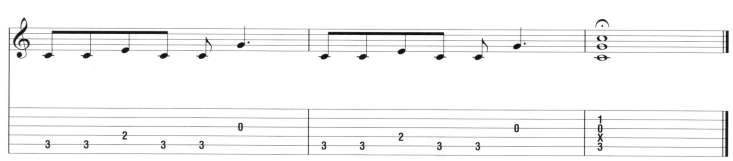

One More Night

Words and Music by Adam Levine, Johan Schuster and Max Martin

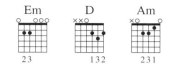

*Capo I

Strum Pattern: 3
Pick Pattern: 3

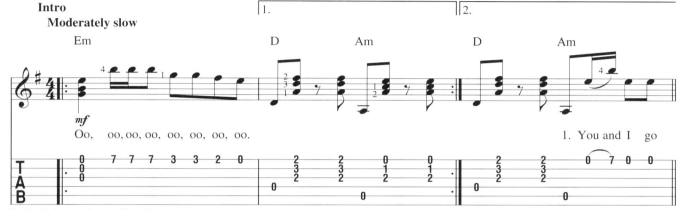

*Optional: To match recording, place capo at 1st fret.

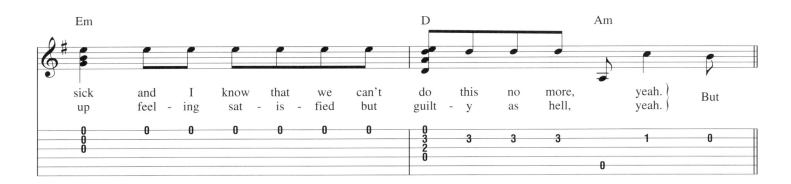

sick and I know that we can't do this no more, yeah.
up feel - ing sat - is - fied but guilt - y as hell, yeah. But

Pre-Chorus

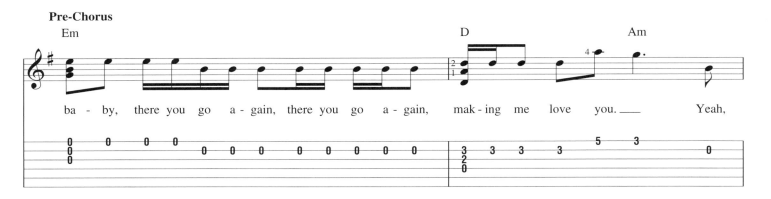

ba - by, there you go a - gain, there you go a - gain, mak - ing me love you. ___ Yeah,

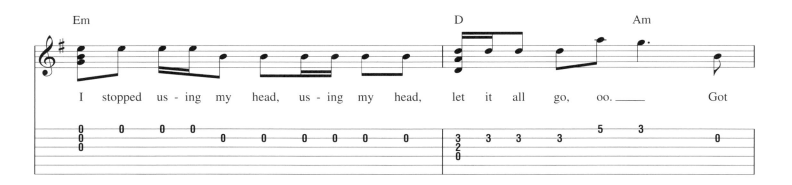

I stopped us - ing my head, us - ing my head, let it all go, oo. ___ Got

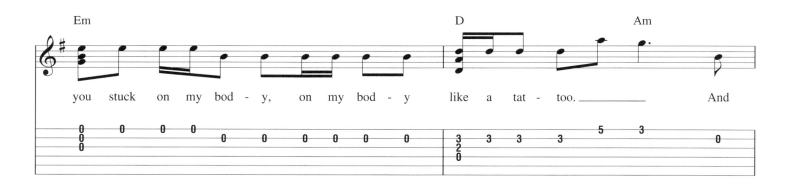

you stuck on my bod - y, on my bod - y like a tat - too. ___ And

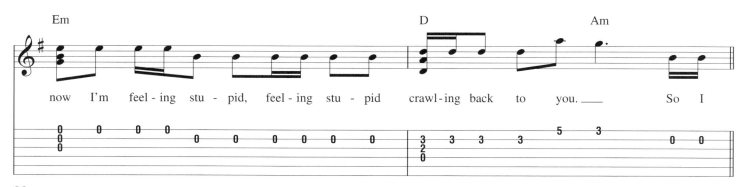

now I'm feel - ing stu - pid, feel - ing stu - pid crawl - ing back to you. ___ So I

Chorus

cross my heart and I hope to die _____ that I'll

on - ly stay with you one more night. _____ And I

know I said it a mil - lion times _____ but I'll

on - ly stay with you one more night. _____ 2. Try to tell you,

Bridge

(Oo,   oo, oo, oo,   oo,   oo,   oo,   oo.

Yeah,   ba - by, give me one   more   night. _____

31

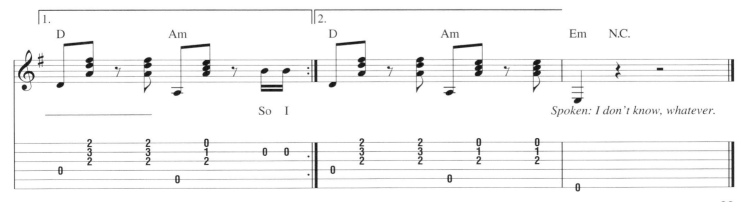

Locked Out of Heaven

Words and Music by Bruno Mars, Ari Levine and Philip Lawrence

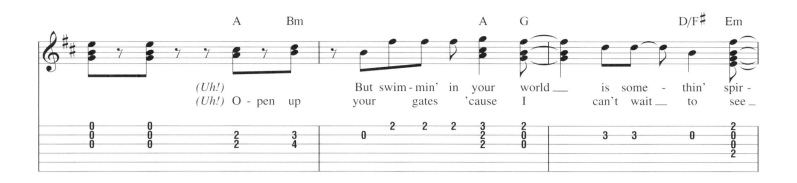

(Uh!)
(Uh!) O- pen up

But swim- min' in your world ___ is some- thin' spir-
your gates 'cause I can't wait ___ to see ___

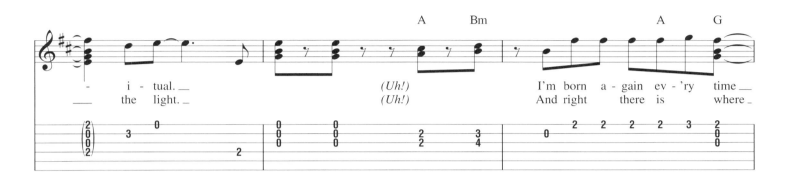

- i - tual. ___
___ the light. ___

(Uh!)
(Uh!)

I'm born a - gain ev - 'ry time ___
And right there is where ___

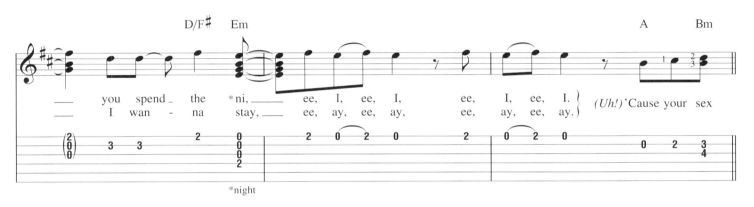

___ you spend ___ the *ni, ___ ee, I, ee, I, ee, I, ee, I. (Uh!)'Cause your sex
___ I wan - na stay, ___ ee, ay, ee, ay, ee, ay, ee, ay.

*night

Pre-Chorus

takes me to par - a - dise. ___ Yeah, your sex takes me to par - a - dise ___ and it**show, ___

**shows

___ oo, oh, ___ oo, oh, ___ oo, ohs. Yeah, ee, yeah, ___ ee, yeah. ___ 'Cause you make me

Madness

Words and Music by Matthew Bellamy

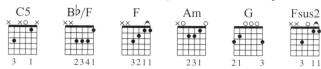

*Tune down 1 step:
(low to high) D-G-C-F-A-D

Strum Pattern: 3
Pick Pattern: 3

Intro
Moderately slow

(M - m - m - m - m - m - m - m-mad, mad, mad,   m - m - m - m - m - m - m - m-mad, mad, mad.)

*Optional: To match recording, tune down 1 step.
**Chord symbols reflect overall harmony.

Verse

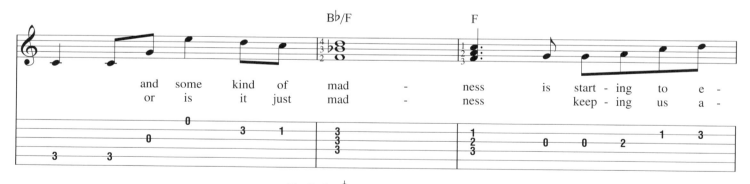

1. I,
2. Now,
3. *Instrumental*

I can't get these mem - 'ries   out of my   mind, _
I need to know   is this   real   love, _

and some kind of mad   -   ness is start - ing to e -
or is it just mad   -   ness keep - ing us a -

To Coda

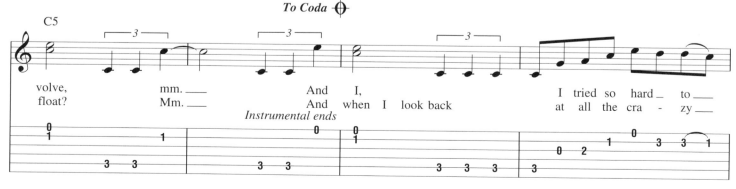

volve,   mm. ___   And I,   I tried so hard _ to _
float?   Mm. ___   And when I look back   at all the cra - zy _
Instrumental ends

© 2012 HEWRATE LIMITED
All Rights in the U.S. and Canada Administered by WB MUSIC CORP.
All Rights Reserved   Used by Permission

38

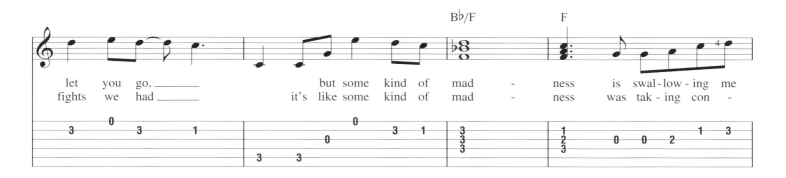

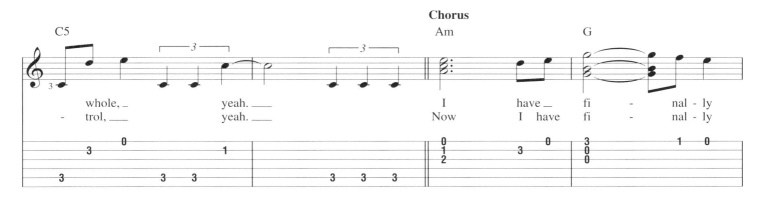

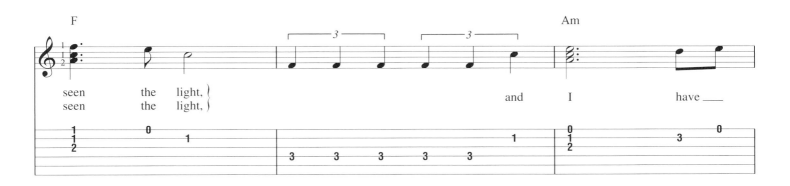

2nd time, D.S. al Coda

*Sung one octave higher.

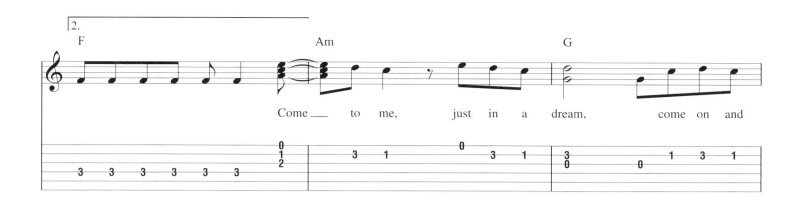

Come ___ to me, just in a dream, come on and

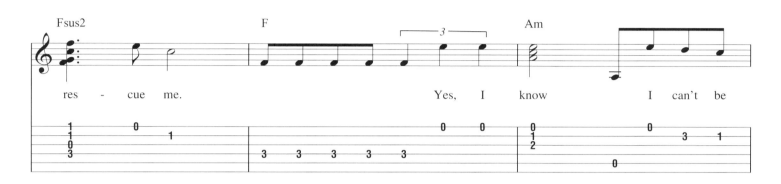

res - cue me. Yes, I know I can't be

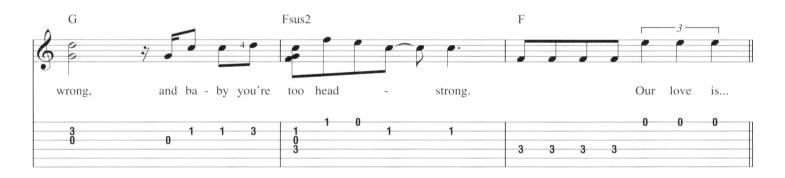

wrong, and ba - by you're too head - strong. Our love is...

Outro

(M - m - m - m - m - m - m - m-mad, mad, mad, m - m - m - m - m - m - m - m-mad, mad, mad,

*Sung as written.

m - m - m - m - m - m - m - m-mad, mad, mad, m - m - m - m - m - m - m - m-mad - ness.)

Skyfall

from the Motion Picture SKYFALL

Words and Music by Adele Adkins and Paul Epworth

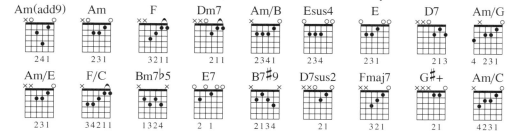

*Capo III

Strum Pattern: 3
Pick Pattern: 3

Intro
Slow

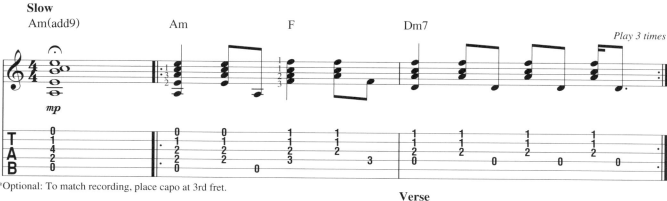

*Optional: To match recording, place capo at 3rd fret.

Verse

1. This is the end. ___

Hold your breath and count ___ to ten. ___ Feel the earth

move and then ___ hear my heart burst ___ a -

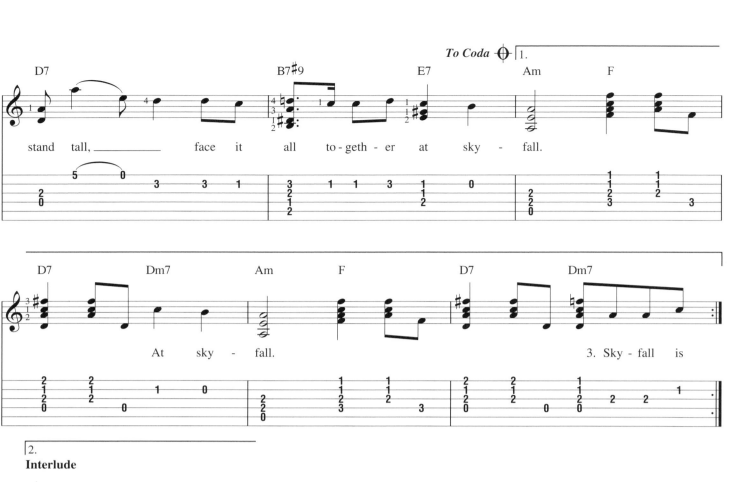

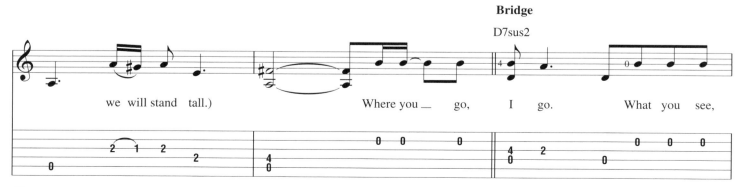

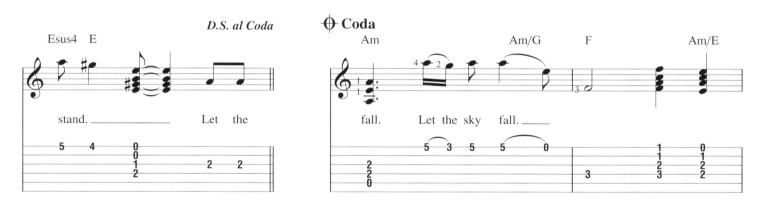

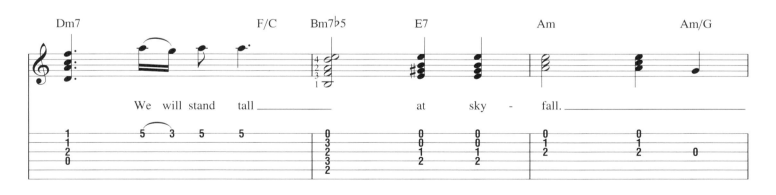

Too Close

Words and Music by Alex Claire and Jim Duguid

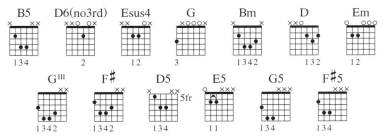

Strum Pattern: 4
Pick Pattern: 4

Intro
Moderately

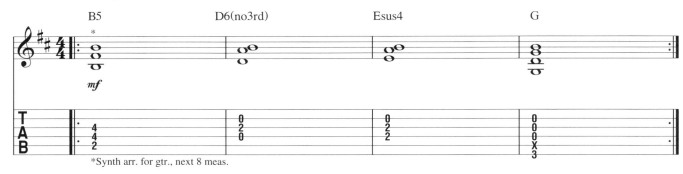

*Synth arr. for gtr., next 8 meas.

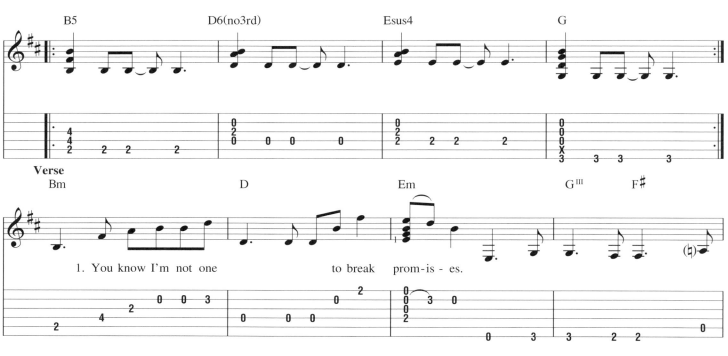

Verse

1. You know I'm not one to break prom-is- es.

I don't wan-na hurt ___ you, but I need to breathe. _

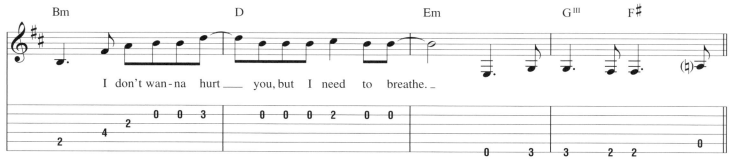

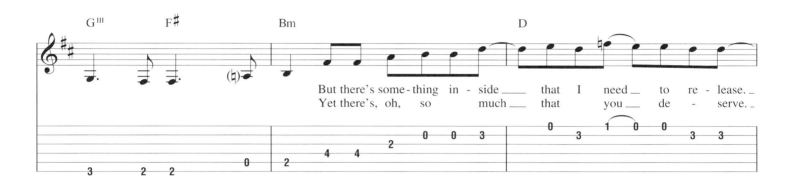

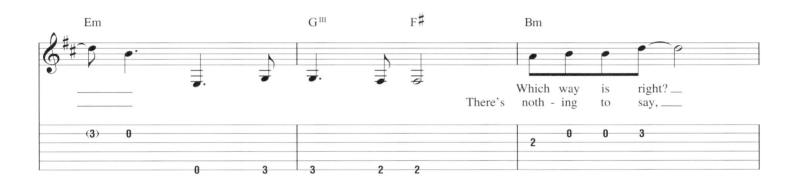

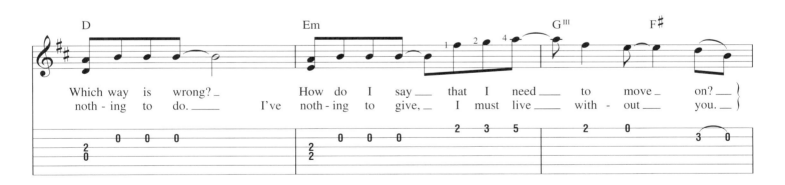

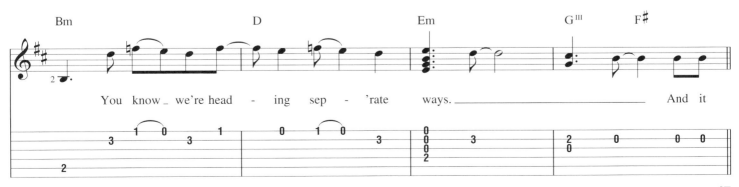

Some Nights

Words and Music by Jeff Bhasker, Andrew Dost, Jack Antonoff and Nate Ruess

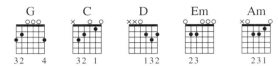

*Capo V

Strum Pattern: 6
Pick Pattern: 6

Chorus
Moderately

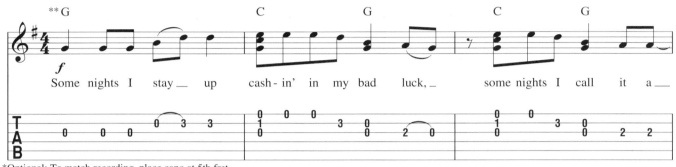

*Optional: To match recording, place capo at 5th fret.
**Harmony implied by vocals, next 8 meas.

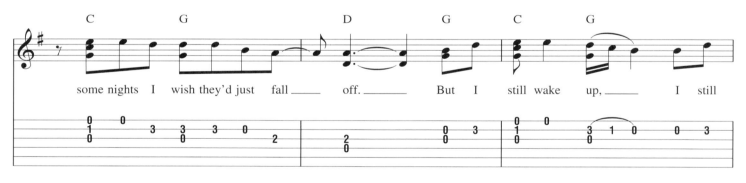

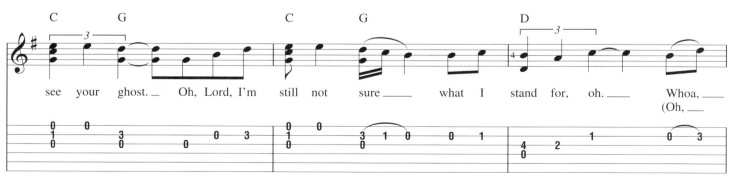

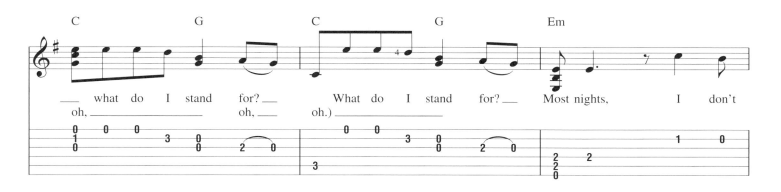

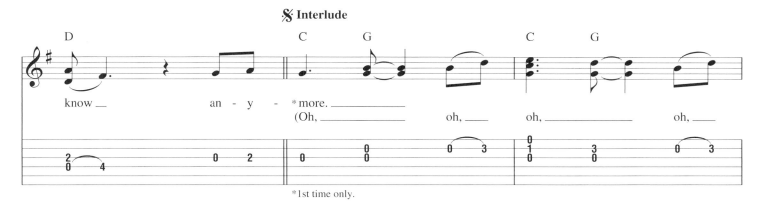

*1st time only.

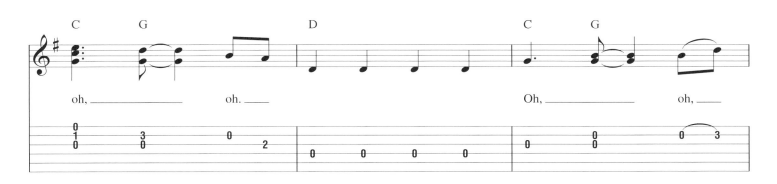

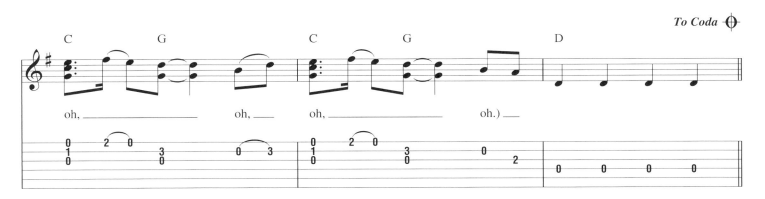

Verse

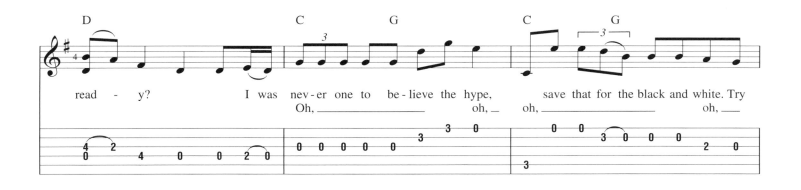

read - y?   I was nev - er one to be - lieve the hype,   save that for the black and white. Try
Oh, _____ oh, _ oh, _____ oh, _

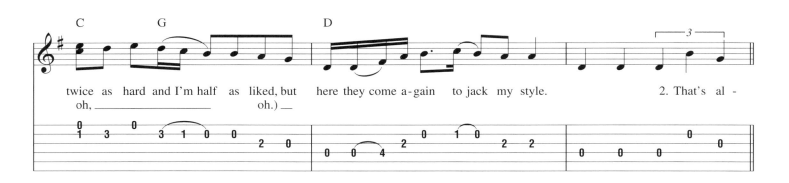

twice as hard and I'm half as liked, but   here they come a - gain to jack my style.   2. That's al -
oh, _____ oh.) _

Verse

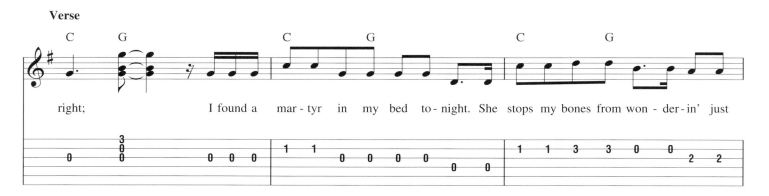

right;   I found a mar - tyr in my bed to - night. She stops my bones from won - der - in' just

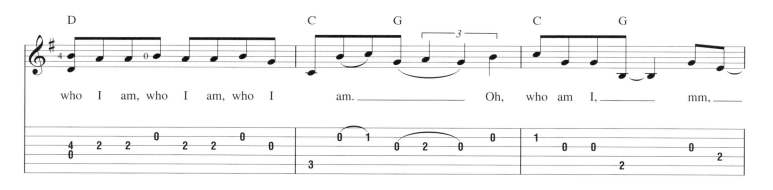

who I am, who I am, who I   am. _____ Oh, who am I, _____ mm, _

Chorus

_   mm. _____   Well, some nights I wish _ that this

all ___ would end _____ 'cause I could use some friends _ for a _____ change. And

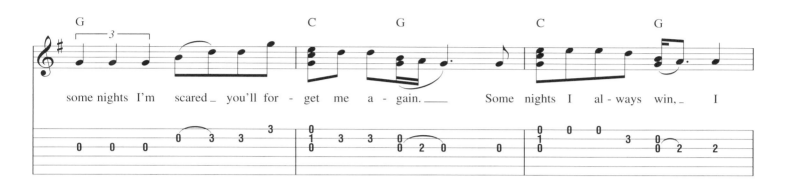

some nights I'm scared _ you'll for - get me a - gain. ___ Some nights I al - ways win, _ I

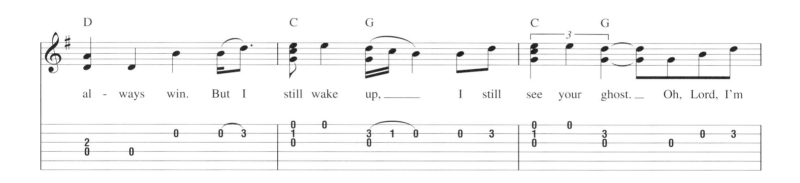

al - ways win. But I still wake up, _____ I still see your ghost. _ Oh, Lord, I'm

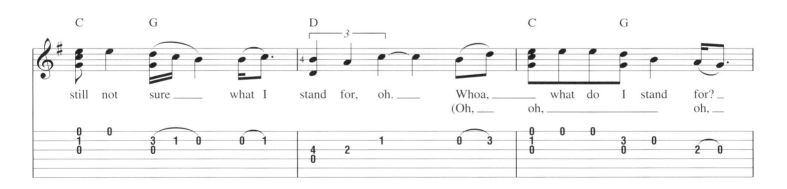

still not sure _____ what I stand for, oh. ___ Whoa, _____ what do I stand for? _
(Oh, _ oh, _____ oh, _

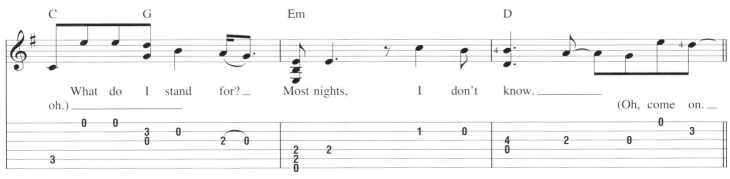

oh.) What do I stand for? _ Most nights, I don't know. _____
(Oh, come on. _

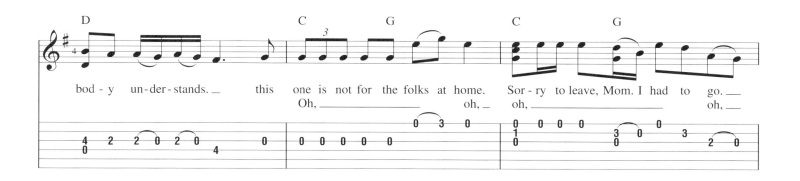

bod - y un-der-stands. ___ this one is not for the folks at home. Sor - ry to leave, Mom. I had to go. ___
Oh, _____ oh, _ oh, _____ oh, ___

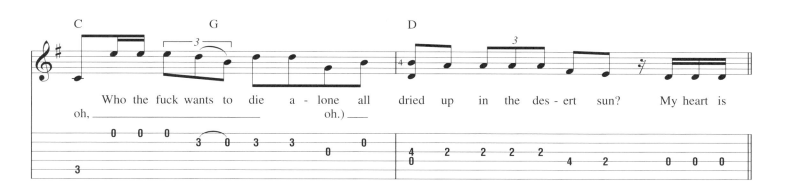

Who the fuck wants to die a - lone all dried up in the des - ert sun? My heart is
oh, _____ oh.) ___

Bridge

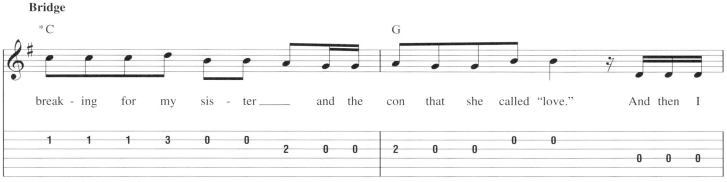

break - ing for my sis - ter _____ and the con that she called "love." And then I

*Let chords ring, next 6 meas.

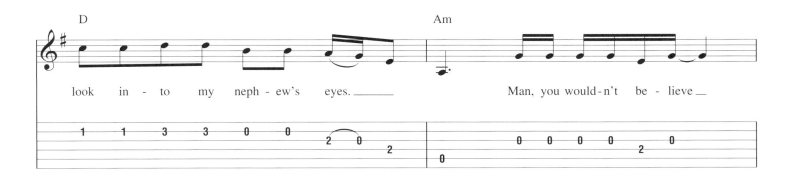

look in - to my neph - ew's eyes. _____ Man, you would-n't be - lieve __

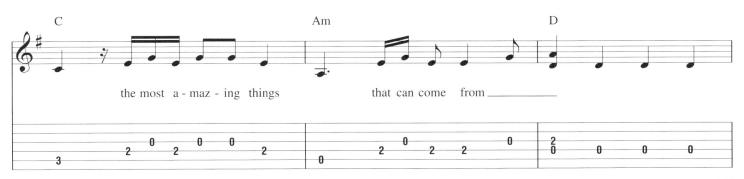

the most a - maz - ing things that can come from _____